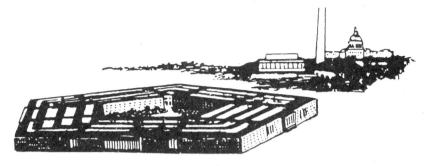

September 11, 2001

The Pentagon Attack

A Tribute in Memory of Workers Who Perished
We Will Never Forget You!

by Nita Scoggan

Royalty Publishing Company
P.O. Box 2125
Bedford, IN 47421

December 21, 2001 – the first shipment of new Limestone
was delivered to the Pentagon on the
Same day as the Olympic torch.

Royalty Publishing Company
P.O. Box 2125
Bedford, IN 47421

Scenes of the Pentagon reproduced from original watercolor
paintings by Nita Scoggan.

ISBN 0-910487-50-2
Library of Congress Catalog Number: Requested

THE PENTAGON

Headquarters of our nation's
Department of Defense
is
The World's Largest Office Building

THEIR WORK

Charged by the U.S. Constitution to:
"Insure domestic tranquility, Provide for the Common
defense, Promote the general welfare, and secure the Blessings
of Liberty to ourselves and our Posterity..."

Sept. 11, 2001 - We Will Never Forget!

The hijacked American Airlines Boeing 757 airliner that slammed into the Pentagon at 9:20 a.m. on September 11, 2001 caused massive damage to the building. The terrorist attack on America's military headquarters killed almost 200 people. At least 72 of the injured were treated at area hospitals, nine were listed in critical condition. Estimated casualties were 800 or less

The plane hit a newly renovated area of the Pentagon and lives were spared as some offices remained empty.

Search and rescue teams spent the night digging through rubble to uncover casualties. Among the first rescue workers were dozens of soldiers from Walter Reed Army Medical Center Medics set up blankets in the Pentagon's center courtyard and treated at least three firemen for smoke inhalation.

Round-the-clock recovery efforts were immediately underway The 3rd U.S. Army Infantry (The Old Guard) was at the Pentagon in force waiting for the flames to subside so that search and rescue work could begin. Several times during the day the search teams approached the rubble only to be called back for safety reasons.

Logistical support was provided by a variety of governmental agencies, including The Old Guard from Fort Myer, Va., the Military District of Washington Engineer Company from Fort Belvoir, Va., the 767th Ordnance Company from Fort McNair, D.C., and the U.S. Army Criminal Investigation Command, also based on Fort Belvoir. They assisted civilian emergency rescue teams that set up operations beyond the Pentagon helipad where the crash occurred. About 300 soldiers of the Virginia National Guard were activated to help in the crisis (Sheftick, Army Link News).

DoD photo by R. D. Ward

President Bush and Secretary of Defense Rumsfeld in front of the crash site at the Pentagon on Sept. 12

U.S. Army photo by SSG John Valceanu

Round-the-Clock Recovery Efforts

Construction – Wartime Miracle

The Pentagon was designed and built in a race against time. It was planned for efficiency, not beauty. Frills and non-functional items were omitted wherever possible. Passenger elevator service was eliminated due to wartime economy.

During the early part of 1941, the President asked Congress for a building to be constructed in or near the District of Columbia, to house the combined military leaders and better coordinate their functions.

Construction began on September 11, 1941, on a 24-hour a day schedule. At one stage, 15,000 men were employed on the job. Work was completed at record speed. Under normal conditions, construction of such a building would take a total of four years. Although constructed in swampy area known as "Hell's Bottom," the Pentagon has held up well, thanks to the structural frame of steel and reinforced concrete, supported by the 41,192 concrete piles on which it rests.

The first office workers began to move in on April 29, 1942, while some construction work was still in progress. There are no escalators to the fifth floor, since there were only four floors in the original design. All construction was completed by January 15, 1943, at a cost of about $83,000,000.

With unification of the Armed Services in 1947, the Pentagon became headquarters for the entire military. Originally designated as the National Military Establishment, the Pentagon later became the Department of Defense.

In the late 1970s an incinerator was installed on the Heating Plant site adjacent to the Pentagon. This incinerator burns nonpulpable classified materials formerly burned elsewhere. Almost 25% of the Pentagon's steam for generating heat and hot water is produced here. About 10 tons of classified waste is burned daily. For every two tons of material burned, one ton of coal is saved.

Pentagon building site -- a swamp!

President Thanks Workers at the Pentagon
The Next Day, Visiting to Inspect the Damage

On September 12, the day following the terrorist attack on the Pentagon, America's military defense headquarters, President Bush came to inspect the damage. Extensive damage was inflicted on the west face of the building, on which the hijacked plane dove at full speed.

"I am so grateful to the people who are working here," the President said. "I want to say thanks to the folks who have given blood to the Red Cross. I want to say thanks for the hundreds of thousands of Americans who pray for the victims and their families.

Secretary Rumsfeld told me ... that he felt the blast shake the Pentagon – even though he was on the other side of the building, the building rocked. And now I know why.

Coming here makes me sad, on the one hand; it also makes me angry. Our country will, however, not be cowed by terrorists, by people who don't share the same values we share, by people who are willing to destroy people's lives because we embrace freedom. The nation mourns, but our government will goon, the country will function. We are on high alert for possible activity.

But, coming here confirms what the Secretary and I both know – that this is a great nation. People here working hard prove it; people out here working their hearts out to answer families' questions, to remove the rubble and debris from this office. I want to thank everybody, not only on this site, but all across America for responding so generously, so kindly, in their prayers, in their contributions of love and their willingness to help in any way they can."

8

We Are Here – No Matter What!

At 0900, Admirals Guter and Lohr, all the aides, EAs, and several AJAGs gathered for the weekly AJAG meeting. Word came in that the World Trade Center had been attacked. We turned on the TV and saw live the scene of horror as the second plane smashed into the South Tower. Everyone in the room let out a collective gasp and stared in momentary disbelief. Quickly Admiral Guter took control and continued the meeting.

Minutes later, a deafening explosion sounded, and a shock wave ripped through the building, shaking the walls and jarring our bones. "We're under attack," and "We've been hit," were the responses after a split second of stunned silence. The plane hit the <u>opposite</u> side of the Pentagon from where our spaces are, and still we were battered around with tremendous force.

Immediately word spread to evacuate. For the most part we were calm and orderly, because we were still in shock over what was happening. We heard shouts and screams "Oh my God!" and "Get the h– out!" Panic was spreading. Many were running in all directions through the corridors. One area of the building lost power, and black with choking smoke. Balls of flame and swarms of debris shot through the affected rings E, D, and C. Word of the fires, and collapsing ceilings and bulkheads spread quickly. Through the mass of people, pressing against each other from every direction, I saw my Admiral ahead. When I reached him, he was calm and resolved.

We finally made it outside through the River Entrance. Ahead I saw the gleaming white Washington Monument. Turning back, I looked on a war zone. Thousands were still pouring from the Pentagon – it seemed black smoke came from half the building.

My mind thought of Pearl Harbor. Was this what those sailors felt – the shock, confusion, surprise, and horror that they had been attacked suddenly and without warning?

Then, soldiers and sailors were running - shouting for doctors, medics, and corpsmen. They had turned the North entrance by the POAC into a morgue and triage to care for the injured. There were many. Word spread that another plane was detected – headed straight for the Pentagon. The ETA was 10 minutes. Orders passed to move father away. Like a scene from a movie, literally thousands of Navy, Marine, Airforce, and Army people ran toward a natural trench along the Potomac River. Thousands threw themselves down, hitting the dirt and taking cover from the imminent second attack.

9

Just as some screamed "Why do we have no air cover?" F-16 fighters from Andrews AFB, their wings visibly packed with missiles, screamed overhead. They flew in circles over the Pentagon and Washington, DC – with the word, we were told, to shoot down ANY airliner that came into the area, no matter how many were onboard. Looking up I thought, "This indeed is war. Thousands of my fellow citizens were dead in New York, my headquarters was burning and collapsing in smoke and rubble before my eyes, and jet fighters were flying combat air cover over our capital for the first time in history."

As we took cover and awaited the imminent second attack, I saw two people collapse from apparent heart attacks. Thankfully it never came.

We were gathered outside the Pentagon, watching it burn, and we felt impotent. We could only help those who were injured, and rage inwardly, pining for a deadly retribution. We had somehow escaped a sneak attack, while too many others working very close to us had paid with their lives. We would never be the same.

That night, Admiral Guter called me at home. His message was simple. "Chris, we're going in tomorrow." "Aye, Sir," I replied. The next morning, at 0545, I headed to my office. Parts of the Pentagon were still burning, smoke billowing upward. Police, military and civilian guards allowed no one in without a building pass. But, DOD workers, military and civilian, headed inside. The courtyard was turned into a makeshift morgue, body bags covering the lawn – laid out in rows like the national cemetery near the Pentagon. The bags weren't full, but ready for what the rescue crews would find later on.

Walking to my office I wasn't alone. Others walked alongside me, faces grim with determination. No one spoke. No one laughed. Smoke and black soot were everywhere. Only the echo of footsteps on the ash-covered floors could be heard throughout. We were sending a message – "You will not frighten us; you will not stop us, no matter what you do."

Chris Ludmer, LT, JAGC, USNR

GOD BLESS AMERICA

DoD photo by R. D. Ward.
The west-facing wall of the Pentagon sags, where a hijacked flight with 64 passengers aboard was purposely crashed into this spot in an act of terrorism.

A Pentagon Survivor's Story

Dr. Betty Mayfield questions why she survived and others nearby did not. "Doc" thanks God, and the military men, whose teamwork efforts enabled her to escape. This is her story.

"At 9:30 a.m., I heard 4-5 unbelievably loud crashing noises. I thought several bombs had gone off. Within seconds, our entire area was engulfed in flames. Glass shattered, lights blew, cabinets fell, ceiling tiles melted - falling like hot cinder balls. I am unable to comprehend how we were left standing when so much around us was destroyed.

My first impulse was to run to a door leading to E-ring, to escape the fire and black smoke. At this moment, LTC Rob Grunewald shouted to all of us to drop to the floor or be overcome by smoke.

Visibility was about one foot, so we formed a human chain, holding onto the foot of the person crawling ahead of us. There was comfort knowing I was not alone. Rob kept shouting for us to keep moving. I knew I had to stay with the group to survive. I felt calmed when I bumped into Col. Phil McNair.

Hot metal pieces from the ceiling were falling on us, and God answered our prayers. The sprinkling system came on and water extinguished the fire, and gave some relief to our lungs.

We crawled about 60-70 feet toward a door leading to the 4th corridor at the B and C rings. I was disheartened when someone yelled that the door wouldn't open. By this time, my lungs were burning – I had trouble breathing. The black smoke was very dense and moving closer to the floor. I realized that I might not get out of the building. My thoughts turned to my family.

Someone shouted we had to make it to a back wall and break a window. I abandoned my crawl and got down on my stomach. The floor was wet but the air was better. I heard breaking glass and learned later that SPC Mike Petrovich and Col. McNair had thrown a printer through a window. It overlooked a service road between the B and C rings.

I was handed a sweater and told to inhale the moisture. One by one, Mike and Phil instructed us to stand up quickly and step up on the windowsill, which was about 3-4 feet from the floor. We were on the second floor and the drop could result in further injuries, but my primary concern was to escape the smoke. They grabbed my wrists and dangled me from the window, and let me drop. I don't know how – but men on the service road caught me, and my feet never touched the ground!

A young Air Force officer rushed me to the center courtyard where the injured were being treated. Then, in the Pentagon Clinic, I was on oxygen until evacuation occurred. A chaplain prayed with me until a van took us to the Urgent Care Center.

Then, I learned an aircraft had struck the Pentagon. I didn't know until two days later that within a few minutes of our escape out of the window, the office in which we were trapped, collapsed. All the time I was trying to escape, I never once thought of the building collapsing.

I thank God for sparing our lives and giving me a way out of the building. I thank God for Rob Grunewald – his commanding voice led us and kept us rapidly moving and working together. I thank God for Mike and Phil who helped save my life. The medical team was superb – and the women at the Urgent Care Center who informed my family that I was a <u>Pentagon survivor</u>.

I would not want to repeat this experience again, but if I had to, I would want to be with military folks such as these I work with at the Pentagon. Their leadership skills and the teamwork effort they organized got us out of the building."
Dr. Betty Mayfield,
Chief, Demographics Office,
ODCSPER, U.S. Army

Local firefighters and rescue personnel join those who escaped
the burning building in rescue efforts Tuesday Sept.11,2001,
U.S. Army Photo by Sgt. Carmen L.Burgess

The Heliport

On September 11, 2001, the hijacked airplane smashed into the Pentagon near the heliport control facilities, on the west side of the building, between the 1st and 2nd floors. On October 11th, President Bush and other dignitaries eulogized the 184 people who were killed during the attack.

Artist's rendering by Nita Scoggan

14

A Prayer Answered – Our Office Didn't Burn!

I worked in room 4E542, on the same side of the Pentagon, by the heliport, that was hit by the hijacked plane. One of our co-workers received a call from his wife that the Trade Center Towers had been struck by a plane – it was thought to be a terrorist attack. My boss, Dr. Zeman, turned on the TV in his office, and we watched in amazement at what was happening in New York. Then, I returned to work at my desk.

About 0935 a call came from Ms. Laura Knight saying she would be late for her 1000 appointment with Dr. Zeman, as her plane had just landed at Reagan National Airport.

Within minutes our room shook violently. At that moment, I turned around to look out the windows. I saw the two windows being blown out. It appeared the bricks came loose. Everyone hit the floor and I yelled "Jesus!" Immediately we were told to get out of the office. I grabbed only my purse. We made our way out of the building. Outside, we saw the fires and realized we would not be going back in the building.

Upon my return to work in a temporary location, I was told over and over that our office had burned completely. However, I told my coworkers that I had prayed that our office would be safe from the fire. I had important papers in the office, including money and checks for a retreat, my personal savings bonds and Christian materials I desperately needed – so I prayed the office would be spared. Everyone thought I was foolish to think this way. In the 1st week in October, OPNAV Security allowed some workers to return and retrieve what was left. They could not wait to tell me that the office was not burned at all!

Offices on our left and right were totally burned. The offices beneath us and above us were completely burned - so I knew the Lord had spared our office because I prayed. Only my tote bag, under my desk, got wet. Everything dried out and was fine including the retreat checks! Seaman Gray told me, "Dottie I know our office was spared because of you. I am going to buy a Bible and start going to church." Lt. Weatherford said, "Dottie that big halo that you have spared our office." Petty Officer Chris Howk said, "Dottie the office did not get burned!" He was overwhelmed because he kept telling me it was impossible, for he saw flames coming out of our office windows on TV. To God be the glory!   *Dottie Powell, Hq. OPNAV.*

(photo by Gary Sheftick)

Soldiers pull casualties from Pentagon

"God Kept Me!"

On September 11th, I overslept that morning. At 8:00 a.m. I called my supervisor to say I would be in at noon. I went back to sleep. At 10:00, my phone rang. It was my friend, Cheryl, who told me that a plane crashed into the Pentagon – and it was my office! I was in shock.

When I returned to work on September 13th, I found out that half of my co-workers and my supervisor were killed. Others were badly burned. Only 4 besides me were not hurt – 3 were sick and one in the restroom. Thank God I overslept because it could have happened to me. God kept me! *Nancy Boyd, HQDA.*

Visting the devistation at the Pentagon, President Bush thank the rescue workers and Pentagon personnel for their diligence through the recent tragedy Sept. 12. White House photo by Eric Draper.

The family members visited the Pentagon on Sept. 15.
U.S. Army photo by SSG John Valceanu

"People Were Shaking & Crying!"

On September 11th, I was told something was going on at the World Trade Towers in New York. I checked my internet and saw the plane hit one tower! I knew there was a TV in the men's locker room on the South Loading Dock and I hurried there. We witnessed the second plane hit the other tower. As we stood there watching, someone said, "This could happen to the Pentagon." Minutes later we felt the building shake – and heard a loud noise. Everyone ran out to the loading dock. People were running and shouting: "We've been hit! We've been hit!"

People rushed back to their offices. Supervisors and security people told us to "stay calm and evacuate." I was praying for the Lord Jesus to help us get out safely. I grabbed my purse and hurried toward the nearest emergency exit door. I forgot that it had been locked for years – since the 1980s when we had a lot of bomb threats. As I came around a corner near that door, I saw it was open! At that moment, I remembered it had been locked. There was no guard was around to open it. I believe an angel opened it for me. Similarly, an angel rolled away the huge stone for the women who went to Jesus' tomb. They needed God's help, and so did I. An angel was sent to help them – and me.

Every body in my area got out safely. It could have been awful if everyone had to use the one stairway to exit. We had no idea part of the building would soon collapse! Outside, in South Parking, we saw a huge cloud of black smoke.

People were shaking and crying. As I rushed to my car, I cried and prayed to our Lord Jesus Christ to save and give peace to all the workers in New York, and the Pentagon.

Pauline Y. Floyd, HQDA

18

It's Not A Small Miracle

The 11th was a rough day, but all of OPNAV N7 got out alive. That's not a small miracle. Probably everyone left alive in the 3rd - 5th corridors has a similar story. The majority of our spaces were located in 5D453. We had moved there about 3-4 months ago – these were the newly renovated spaces.

Like every other American, we were watching the footage from the World Towers. Things had settled down a bit after the President's message, and a few bubbas had mentioned the Pentagon White House and the Capitol Building were probably targets. We knew things had just changed for the worse and that the day would be a long one in the Pentagon.

Suddenly, the building jumped 2-3 inches. Everyone instinctively looked out. We had probably 20-30 windows, each about 4-feet across, in our spaces. We saw nothing but a fireball. None of the glass broke, the lights stayed on, and the computers ran for a few more seconds. In the corner, some accoustic roofing fell down, but that was all the damage.

It takes a few seconds to process that kind of information. You realize that a plane probably just slammed into the Pentagon. You want to call home and tell everyone you're okay. You want to grab your computer, wallet and keys that are 10-feet away. But you decide to leave everything and just get out.

Everyone came to that conclusion at the same time and we started heading to the door. About 100 of us have an office there, and we walked/ran out. You could see the smoke starting to filter in from the E-ring – then people starting to exit the E-ring. Only about 20 folks came from that direction. When the last one came through, the smoke was too thick for them to see. They came out holding hands to keep everyone together and crouched low to the ground. They followed our shouting voices and eventually broke into the clear.

We exited to the center of the Pentagon and went out into the parking lot. It'll be a long time before I forget that smell. We all looked towards the Capitol building and the White House, relieved not to see black plumes of smoke there. Only later did we learn that the aircraft had circled above those buildings before crashing into the Pentagon.

When we left our office, it was still intact. However, the plane had traveled directly under us on the first and second floors.

When you look at the collapsed E-ring, you can see our windows behind the debris. For the first two days you could see someone's potted plant through the window. Then - you couldn't. Our floor completely collapsed and took everything with it. You don't realize how much you have invested in an office until it's gone.

Like you've heard – the new construction probably saved hundreds of lives. The reinforced concrete walls slowed the airplane. The outer, blast-proof windows contained the blast and allowed us to exit with only two slight injuries instead of multiple wounds from flying glass. We're lucky to be alive and we know it. Please pray for all the families, especially those in New York.   *Cdr Don Braswell, USN, N78.*

President Bush pays a surprise visit to the Pentagon

DoD photo by R. D. Ward.

President shakes hands with Air Force Staff Sgt. Amy Hunter on Sept. 17, 2001.

DoD photo by Helene C. Stikkel.

President thanks Pentagon personnel for their dedication and perseverance.

Pentagon Renovation Saved Lives

The structural changes made in a newly renovated area of the Pentagon where the hijacked jetliner crashed provided increased protection – and reduced the number of casualties.

The changes included steel beams that ran through all five floors of the Pentagon, said Lee Evey, the Pentagon renovation program manager. The beams strengthened walls around the newly installed blast-resistant windows and safety.

Additionally, there was the Kevlar-like cloth, made up of the same material as bulletproof vests, which prevented debris from becoming shrapnel, Evey said.

"This was a terrible tragedy ... but if we had not undergone the effort to make these changes, the outcome could've been a lot worse," Evey said (Triggs, 9/15/01, Army Link News).

A contract was issued to include repairs to areas with water and smoke damage, that occurred when flames from the crash continuously burned through the night and into the morning.

The damaged wedge sections have to be torn down, cleared and rebuilt, and that could take about 18 months. However, the contract does not include the cost to repair the wedge that collapsed after the terrorist attack, Evey said.

A current concern at the building is the growth of mold and mildew caused by water poured into fires, Evey said. The building's air is tested extensively "to ensure that it's a healthy work environment." Historical documents in the renovated library are unharmed, he added (Gilmore/AFIS, 10/3/01, defenselink.mil).

Aerial photograph of the Pentagon taken on Sept.14, 2001, shows some of the destruction.

DoD photo by R. D. Ward

President Bush Pays Tribute at the Pentagon Memorial Service of Remembrance

On October 11, 2001, President Bush thanked a throng of thousands at the Pentagon ceremony – including the first lady, his Cabinet, congressional leaders, and victims' relatives. A red rose was placed on the seat of each relative of the victims.

"We have come here to pay our respects to 125 men and women who died in the service of America. We also remember 64 passengers on a hijacked plane; those men and women, boys and girls who fell into the hands of evildoers, and also died here exactly one month ago.

On September 11th, great sorrow came to our country. And from that sorrow has come great resolve. Today, we are a nation awakened to the evil of terrorism, and determined to destroy it. That work began the moment we were attacked; and it will continue until justice is delivered.

Americans are returning, as we must, to the normal pursuits of life ...But we know that if you lost a son or daughter here, or a husband, or a wife, or a mom or dad, life will never again be as it was. The loss was sudden, and hard, and permanent. So difficult to explain. So difficult to accept ...

One life touches so many others. One death can leave sorrow that seems almost unbearable. But, to all of you who lost someone here, I want to say: You are not alone. The American people will never forget the cruelty that was done here and in New York, and in the sky over Pennsylvania.

We will never forget all the innocent people killed by the hatred of a few. We know the loneliness you feel in your loss. The entire nation ...shares your sadness. And we pray for you and your loves ones. And we will always honor their memory.

The hijackers were instruments of evil who died in vain. Behind them is a cult of evil which seeks to harm the innocent and thrives on human suffering. Theirs is the worst kind of cruelty, the cruelty that is fed, not weakened, by tears. There is the worst kind of violence, pure malice, while daring to claim the authority of God. We cannot fully understand the designs and power of evil. It is enough to know that evil, like goodness, exists. And in the terrorists, evil has found a willing servant.

... <u>And the attack on the Pentagon ... was more symbolic than they knew. It was on another September 11th – September 11th 1941 – that construction on this building first began.</u> America was just then awakening to another menace: The Nazi terror in Europe.

On that very night, President Franklin Roosevelt spoke to the nation. "The danger," he warned, "has long ceased to be a mere possibility. The danger is here now ..."

For us too, in the year 2001, an enemy has emerged that rejects every limit of law, morality, and religion. The terrorists have no true home in any country ... they dwell in dark corners of earth. And there, we will find them.

This week, I have called ... the Armed Forces into action. One by one, we are eliminating power centers of a regime that harbors al Qaeda terrorists. We gave that regime a choice: turn over the terrorists, or face your ruin. They chose unwisely.

The Taliban regime has brought nothing but fear and misery to the people of Afghanistan. These rulers call themselves holy men, even with their record of drawing money from heroin trafficking. They consider themselves pious and devout, while subjecting women to fierce brutality. The Taliban allied itself with murderers and gave them shelter. But today, for al Qaeda and the Taliban, there is no shelter.

As Americans did 60 years ago, we have entered a struggle of uncertain duration. But now, as then, we can be certain of the outcome ... We have a unified country. We have the patience to fight and win on many fronts: Blocking terrorist plans, seizing their funds, arresting their networks, disrupting communications opposing their sponsors.

And we have one more great asset in this cause: the brave men and women of the United States military.

You've responded to a great emergency with calm and courage. And for that, your country honors you. A Commander-in-Chief must know must know that he can count on the skill and readiness of servicemen and women at every point in the chain of command. You have given me that confidence.

And I give you these commitments. The wound to this building will not be forgotten, but it will be repaired. Brick by brick, we will quickly rebuilt the Pentagon. In the missions ahead for the military, you will have everything you need, every resource, every weapon – every means to assure full victory for the United States and the cause of freedom.

And I pledge to you that America will never relent on this war against terror. There will be times of swift, dramatic action. There will be times of steady, quiet progress. Over time, with patience, and precision, the terrorists will be pursued. They will be isolated, surrounded, cornered, until there is no place to run, or hide, or rest.

As military and civilian personnel in the Pentagon, you are an important part of the struggle we have entered. You know the risks of your calling, and you have willingly accepted them. You believe in our country, and our country believes in you.

Within sight of this building is Arlington Cemetery, the final resting place of many thousands who died for our country over the generations. Enemies of America have now added to these graves, and they wish to add more. Unlike our enemies, we value every life, and we mourn every loss.

Yet, we are not afraid. Our cause is just, and worthy of sacrifice. Our nation is strong of heart, firm of purpose. Inspired by all the courage that has come before, we will meet our moment and we will prevail.

May God bless you all, and may God bless America."

DoD photo by R. D. Ward.

President Bush and first lady wave the flag and sing "God Bless America" at the Pentagon memorial service

Fire fighters and military personnel unfurl
a large American Flag from the roof of the Pentagon.

DoD photo by R. D. Ward.

DoD photo by R. D. Ward.

The American Flag, draped over the wall of the Pentagon
is lowered on Oct. 11, 2001.

DoD photo by Helene Stikkel

Pentagon employees read short biographies of those killed
in the Sept. 11th terrorist attack during a memorial service
at the Pentagon on Oct. 11, 2001.

Family Members of victims, killed during the Sept. 11th terrorist attack, Build A Memorial to their loved ones outside the damaged building.

DoD photo by John Valceanu, US Army

Family Members Build Memorial

Former Foreign Minister of the USSR Shevardnadze Sees Pentagon Damage and Pledges To Fight Terrorism

On October 5, 2001, U.S. Deputy Defense Secretary Paul D. Wolfowitz and Georgian President Eduard Shevardnadze pledged mutual support in the fight against global terrorism, at a Pentagon news conference.

Shevardnadze was first taken to see the damaged sections of the Pentagon's west wall. Afterward, he attended a military honors ceremony and then entered the Defense Department's headquarters for a 45-minute meeting with Wolfowitz.

Wolfowitz called the meeting "very successful ...Georgia was one of the first countries to offer its full and unconditional support to the United States in the fight against terrorism." He noted the United States would be working with Georgia in the days and months ahead "in efforts to secure that country's borders and its population from terrorism."

Shevardnadze noted that his talks with Wolfowitz were conducted "in the same spirit of good will and partnership" as his prior discussions with President Bush.

"Our two countries, together with friends, must join efforts to fight global terrorism," he said. Shevardnadze added while he and Wolfowitz didn't necessarily discuss specific Georgian support, the use of his country's airspace was a possibility.

(Gilmore/AFIS/Oct52001, defenselink.mil).

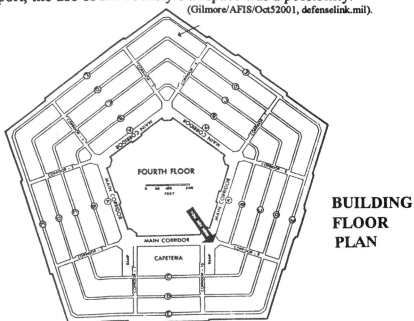

BUILDING FLOOR PLAN

"Whom shall I send and who will go for us? . . .
Here am I: send me." Isaiah 6:8 *by Woodi Ishmael*

God Bless America

God bless America,
Land that I love,
Stand beside her—
And guide her—
Through the night with a light
from above;
From the mountains,
To the prairies—
To the oceans—
White with foam,
God bless America,
My home sweet home,
God bless America,
My home sweet home.

Statistical Tidbits

The Pentagon is one of the world's largest office buildings, on a total land area of 583 acres. It houses more than 24,000 people.

Cleaning the 83–acres of offices is accomplished at night–it is a gigantic job. About 100–acres of asphalt, and ceramic tile floor has to be kept scrubbed, waxed and buffed. The 7,748 windows must be cleaned. It was reported that more than 175,000 rolls of toilet paper, 35 million paper towels and 12,500 quarts of liquid hand soap were used annually, in cleaning the 280 restrooms.

Work crews constantly strive to keep the Pentagon and the 175–acre area neat and clean. Surrounding the building are 51/2 acres of sidewalks, and over 82 acres of roadways, which are cleaned with power equipment.

Interesting facts about the building:

Stairways	150
Escalators	19
Elevators	13
Rest rooms	280
Fixtures	4,900
Drinking fountains	685
Electric clocks	4,200
Light fixtures	65,000
Daily lamp replacements	1,000
Windows	7,748
Glass area	309,276 sq.ft.
equals	7.1 acres
Parking space (acres)	67
Capacity (vehicles)	10,000
Office space (sq.ft.)	3,705,793

Dept. Of Defense photo.

Observing the 50th Anniversary of the Department of Defense
Secretary of Defense William Cohen (standing right) and General Joseph Ralston, U.S. Air Force, Vice Chairman of the Joint Chiefs of Staff, review passing honor guards during Pentagon ceremonies, September 17, 1997.

The Pentagon designated a
A NATIONAL HISTORIC LANDMARK
1992